C J ZYCK

LET FREEDOM REIGN

ODE TO THE SEMIQUINCENTENNIAL OF
THE DECLARATION OF INDEPENDENCE
AN ECLECTIC COLLECTION OF POEMS
VOLUME ONE

* * ** * ** * ** * ** * ** * ** * *

DEDICATION

Dedicated in memory of the citizen Patriots who defended the United States of America's Constitution, in making the ultimate sacrifice to protect the natural rights inherent to free humans, among them life, liberty, and the pursuit of happiness.

To the citizens in service of the military, public office, teachers, firefighters, clinical, hospital, law and order, and all of the public employees who observe and maintain the well-being of the human condition, and the quality of life, of the people, by the people, for the people.

In Celebration of the Land of the Free and the Home of the Brave.

FOREWORD

"Ask not what your country can do for you - ask what you can do for your country."
    – John F. Kennedy

"Where liberty dwells, there is my country."
    – Benjamin Franklin

"I only regret that I have but one life to lose for my country."
    – Nathan Hale

"The only thing we have to fear, is fear itself."
    – Franklin Delano Roosevelt

"Truth will ultimately prevail when there are pains to bring it to light."
    – George Washington

TABLE OF CONTENTS

TABLE OF CONTENTS

Empty Pad

I come home to sit
   with a cigarette, a yard of beer,
   a beer belly, no money,

Here I am, dear, love me,
   my pencil broke,
   the page screams for ideas

I sit here feeble, waiting
   for you to come to me
   hopeless yet not myself apathetic

I am a liar, filled with
   conceit, self-disgust
   you are my muse

Have I anything to give?
   no change if behind time,
   a happiness of fun is up for grabs

Pay me a million dollars
   because I am a disgusting
   degenerate, rolling in the pen

I suck because
   I   am below life
I   am   everything, brother, a man

An oar in the channel of thoughts
the click, clock, wood, tocks
   on without stop,

And the woman who lives above me
     Who stomps on the floor
         must want to be with me

I stomp my feet for you,

I stomp my feet only
    for you!

The knock on the floor above
    from the heels of hard, short
    steps. The cough of my

friend, my roommate
    cough, cough, are
    because of theirs, I will do it.

There is a planet, a plate, a bowl
    ingredients mixing with the folds of years
    grievances, a toll each generation pays

get over yourself to give the take
    Turbulence makes peace in the mirror
    I'm the tougher, by the way.

Enlightenment

Set In Ways Of Common Sense
out of the crisis of human history
Privilege undermines the privileged
to even the playing field
a league formed by heritage
did ways to a means for a few
breaking the mold of ancestral dogma
with what is why virtuous when existence
Make, take, wake to human behavior
tides rise, crest onto shores, and the ebb and flow
tides recede, unveiling what was hidden
Within the ocean's depths
the shell of history discovers
Unknowns, anyhow, reshaping the stories
told myth-laden, superstitious lies
Of privilege earned through deceitful
manipulation, contempt for human existence
Every mind has its own universe
solitary thoughts of the way people live life
The desire to inspire or to oppress
solitary in action to preserve, protect
The desire for inclusion upholds pluralism
secular state separates from dictatorial monotheism
The righteousness of equality
suppresses the primitive impulses
of injustice, greed, avarice
to exploit, demean, destroy
the common rule of love and order
mitigated by peers based on reason, rationale, and facts
Throw out the hypocrisy of criminality
reward integrity, principled behavior adheres
to the well-being of the human condition
individuals collectively reflect diversity
Plurality is human identity
no question, the disclosure is unanimous

from the point of creation
no one lifetime can discern all of
Existence, no one mind contains all
knowledge to a clear conscience
Generations contribute to the growth
to the progress through experience
Tender critical thought surfaces
the elixir of love for being
Created equal for opportunity,
justice, the pursuit is fulfillment
Realization closer to the natural model
of how living is to be shared, cherished,
Respected by ~ we, the people of the United States
of America for which it stands
One Nation resulting from
Enlightenment.

Biblical times
gave slavery a free
pass
The strife of serfs, peasants, and the disenfranchised
the oppression, discrimination
ostracization fed by indifference
the evil of the callous disrespect of the human
condition exemplified most strikingly
by imperialism inspired, by a renaissance,
the rediscovery of ancient
texts, turned into a marketing campaign
for the myths and superstitions
to proselytize dictatorship
as a counter to scientific discovery,
the hints of truth about Nature are
Enlightenment after the atrocities
of imperial expansion resulting
in the holocaust of the Aztecs,
Mayan, Inca Empires,
Native Americans faced
despotic greed from the

Throne of England to its
cotton fields, plantations of
the colonies, where freedom
was won, for the white man
to govern himself, detaching
from the holy throne, the
dictatorship of monotheism

The Enlightenment usurps a
Renaissance with the promise
Of life, liberty, and the pursuit
of happiness, the prologue
for a noble movement to come
once independence was secured
In 1776,
Abolitionist Benjamin Franklin
John Adams, the recalcitrant Thomas
Jefferson of the Continental Congress; hear the cry of
"Live free or die!", echoing: "Give me liberty,
or give me death," Patrick Henry
    Thomas Paine defines the Crisis,
makes the argument for
    Common Sense
"Don't Tread On Me"
    Crispus Atticus the first
Colonist rebel to fall, a Black
Bostonian, a Patriot, sheds
Blood, immortalized
    The fascism of America,
the Antebellum South with
    their 'peculiar institution'
No more free passes on slavery
Where all men are created equal
Civil War in the Eighteen-Sixties
Civil Rights movement in the Nineteen-Sixties
Civil unrest in the fifties of both centuries in
the land of the free, home of the brave
    the first two full centuries

The first quarter century was a fight for independence
in the past quarter century
rekindles the conflict of
the brutish, primitive, ignorant
Ancestral Ancient Past, against
the revealing of its nature
to itself, the clarity of right
and wrong, injustices to resolve
methods of understanding
Who we are, recognizing our
vast similarities that define us as
one existence, to live in full rights
of our individual liberties, to
pursue happiness exploring
expressing our distinguishing
unique, authentic selves
    The constitutional American
is born free, is the bravest of,
    in the fight -
Holocausts occur when the
encroachment of aggressors
define themselves as pure,
    or chosen, any contrivance for
        a manifest destiny
Calculated choreography
for exploitation of
Indigenous or prosperous minorities
    Restitution by the casino over
the sacred lands, isolation on
    Indian reservations, Japanese internment
camps, the public housing slums
to hold a people down, who are
punched down by bigots when
Black communities rise, Tulsa 1921, Harlem Renaissance
    on the wave of the roaring twenties
The egregious promise of wealth for
everyone to invest in the stock market to get rich
quick, racism, Jim Crow, and the height of

terrorist membership of five
million adorning white sheets in
1925, the Black Thursday of the Great Depression
   Look around, the suffragettes
gaining the vote in 1919, women
smoke, swear in public,
   the abusive alcoholic men.
Reformed teetotalers?

Prohibition brought up Capone, who
   murdered a man in Massachusetts
sought exile in Chicago in 1920, the
   year of the first domestic terrorist
attack. A horse-drawn wagon on Wall Street,
the noon hour detonation was premature,
avoiding mass murder.
Shrapnel holes remain to replay
on the Morgan Stanley building
   one hundred years, several
terrorist attacks later, the new
boss is the same as the old boss,
greed-fascist against the promise
of the idea embodied in both
The Declaration of Independence
hand in hand with the invisible
hand of innovation from the
free marketplace of ideas, after
advances of civil rights,
Women's Rights, feminism knocking on
the glass ceiling began cracking
   when the equal rights amendment
the meaning of choice,
      the power of 'me too'
in business, in politics, in life, is short of
progress achieved across the globe!
   The privilege of those ensconced from
their *criminality* against humanity
The overreach of *Citizen's United* is

iconoclastic in a society
divided, the free pass of *slavery*
is permitted, a contradiction
when an *owned* corporation
 granted citizen status is
 a violation of the law, to own a citizen
of the idiot who cosplays as a dick-King
is praised as a holy savior
by the hypocritical vultures of prosperity
evangelism. A line is drawn
the time reaches dawn
  to vanquish the primitive
    dysfunction from
the exploitive Piscean epoch
  making their last stand of hoarding
 abundance from the browbeating, bullying violence
  in the name of manifest destiny
Ineptitude, while the virtuous life
Loving-kindness continuously reaches out
with empathy, compassionate
understanding brand – the fuse of
enlightenment once ignited burns bright
 in righteousness for all humankind.
  To love who you love,
              free from fear,
of openly sharing who we are
    revealing ourselves to ourselves
reaches the heart of our common
          mutual
              existence.
Enlightenment,
          for better and for worse,

                    to forge a more
                  perfect **Union**!!!

Benjamin Franklin Sage

Let one citizen's rights be violated
systematically everyone's rights are violated
    for a free mind to speak the truth
of reality consistent with solid reason,
rationale critical thinking to question everything
in light of the twisted nonsense of the feeble-minded

With wit and wisdom to win the day
imagining a better world to stray
    to steal Prometheus' fire
taking the thunder by conducting
the lightning with a key and a kite
someday to ignite the stove of his invention

The oldest of the delegates, respected
for more than his mind, his manly delights
    sophisticate to degenerate, playfully
did he participate, the spreading of thought
convincing in hold of the helm of independence
the sage of natural rights spun infectious insights

Breaking the submissive bonds of intimidation
from the wealth and power of a King, the tyrant of all
    blue, green; the air we breathe is given freely,
a diplomat to befriend the powers to obtain
what had never been, simmering within many
colonists' hearts, the sage is held in esteem
uniting the colonies of America was his dream,
    it's ours to keep if we can!

Sprinkles Of Whitman *

Orators of freedom of human autonomy
   cut out the form of thought to practice
Guard against your laziness to self-inform
   educate on experience, example
verse and rhyme, converse with the divine
   Be not curious about beyond experience
to build an aesthetic, create a great society
   It is not to be curious about oneself solely
I am curious about all, curious to others' uniqueness
   In the rotunda of the White House
finding the illustrious scenes
   of governance of a new breed in human history
The free speakers of the free marketplace
   of ideas, speak nothing of the beginning
or the end, for the end is intended as is the
   beginning, for all that matters, is the turn
of time, as it passes here and now,
   the continuous, spontaneous instant;
the irrational primitive societal structure
   of irrational behavior, anchored in ignorance
the primal urge demands the disciplines of education
   enforce the practice of civility where equals
display, share their unique and common selves
   contributing what is needed now and forever
- diversity -

Orators from the Continental Congress. Adams, Franklin
   the writings of Jefferson, Paine, to harken the fair
citizens of a concept of unalienable rights, inherited from
   the moment of consciousness, "Cogito, ergo sum," René
Descartes. The fallen soldier, handsome, joyous, taken from us,
the son from the mother, the husband from the wife, the dear
friend from a dear friend. Failing to fetch me at first keep
   encouraged, Missing me one place search another, I stop
somewhere waiting for you.

(*Contains material in the public domain)

For God And Country: Peace On Earth

If the Middle East
   Might be able to
   Give up the

I think about those young
   People who die in wars
   Sacrificing their lives
   For God and country
   How they leave

Their young spouses
   With their young children
   And die to protect their
   Safety, their happiness,
   Though their loved ones are sad

With their loss
   I find I must commit to
   Living a long life
   Discovering a way
   To end war

sacrifice
   in my life
   what they had lost
   in their pursuits
   for the rest of us to live

A long life
   to end
   all war
   for those
   who remain.

The Proof Of The Murder

the miracle of life
   exists right before
   your eyes,
    the grace, power,
    the ultimate truth
    of nature,
    you value
Has your monetary riches,
  destroying what is
  truly precious in exchange
for your fleeting glory?

You are empty,
    meaningless,
you are beyond the crazy
    of the human experience.
You are insane,
    criminal
in great need of reprimanding

Banishment if you
   do not reconcile
   your ways
    monetary harvester.

I say the world
   the same
    it shivers, quivers
   sending itself into
   oblivion,
   I say I am the
same as I encounter,

charge bringing myself
   to my same self, different
   but the same as I've

I do not entirely
   bound up into a ball
   I do not entirely
   grow myself up
   to become who I am
   I am to be what
   I am as what

I decide as it is
   what you decide
   what you become
   the walls   don't bark
        back

I Might Wake

   Up Dead Sometime
only mealy dirt
   worms, maggots feasting

on my flesh, mortal tissues
   Morbid to look
   forward to
disintegrating

   The release is
   of my life,
If I'm lucky
   enough

   to know,

or not to know
I might wake up
dead sometime

Sometime
Anytime,
Space time,
Our time,
Fun time,
Hope time,
Compassion
love time,
while we
were alive
time

Moments So Truthful They Eternally Shine

I am just shocked, stunned
  by the loveliness of life
truth is reality
  we will see it
Nature, we are revealing
  ourselves in moments
      through the
  moments organic,
 own the moment
so truthful through
  presence alive
  they eternally shine
in waves, speak bending time
  impressions expressions
    eternally shine.

Commander of Love

You are the sergeant-at-arms
    of all angels
You are certain they all have bows
    and "arrows for hearts"
In one command, the tenant angels
    let fly a blanket of love
        down upon earth
        then singing an angel's hail to you:
    "You give love freely,
        sharing all, endlessly"
I am your quartermaster
    who stands proudly by your side.
I see the world as you cannot
I see the blisters and scars
soaring through it, I see
    zillions of times not achieved
  many more moments
    of hopes to arrive.
I am generous
    offering my goodness
  my best of soul
    I know I cannot
  always deliver
my love shines
  beyond boundaries
    surpassed,
    environment, focus on the human mind.
Give me your love
  dear one,
    my love, through hand
  heart
I will exchange,
    time will be witness
    to my honor
them who wear

uniforms   realities in this one
are clowns of   truth's beliefs
  yes, god, I will   in order to speak
  be a frog in   my next lifetime

  my next lifetime

In order to speak
  truths, beliefs, and
  realities in this one.

I dream of how well
I would take care of my
family, how well I'd
treat my friends
sipping another glass of
wine, I hold this unforgiving
empty pink slip in my
hand.
Life is short,
You get to know People,
You think about them.
I think I'm fortunate to know you!
            ~ Lucky, not money, of course
              (in a healing sense, not in a money sense)
I think you happen to rule the world.
  (Ok, is my point getting across?)
  Furthermore . . .! @! #? WWW.++
***** "+"

        HEART
          +
        CHEER'S
        ALL DAY thin night
        Ń)) DARK
        "+")☺) Again, moon dark
              Moonlit
                    ME -
                        Commander of

Love.

In Matters Of Human Survival *

Agitate! Agitate!
    The words of the peaceful protester
Civil disobedience, the rights of dutiful
        Americans, protest, sing it out loud
Abolitionists from the thirteen colonies, then to
        thirty-four states, bleeding Kansas,
Abolitionists of isolationists, from the sinking
        of the Lusitania, to a surprise attack
        of Pearl Harbor, propelling forty-eight states
All of these wars were fought with rights
        to life, liberty, and freedom in the balance
United States of America, the fierce experiment
        The Declaration of Independence established
        no one is above the law and order of
A morally just land of the free
        home of the brave: The brave who gave
        their conviction of freedom for all, many
Made the ultimate sacrifice, for you and me
        to keep the pursuit of happiness free
In action, to defeat tyranny with conflict
        the force multiplier of having each other's backs
        the pluralism of backs enforcing their
Unity to dissolve the enemy who are aligned against
        humanity, two tyrants, two claims
        of racial superiority, two menacing Monarchies,
        two alarms of their sovereignty to rule
        the conduits for all humankind to god.

Agitate! Agitate!
Abolitionists of fascism in politics
        of fear, the Red Scare, propagated
        by xenophobic politicians, the
Buck stops here, proliferates to a
        marketing campaign of a 'domino effect,'
        defend against the Red Scare, spread

of Communism will threaten 'our way of life'
Where? Pockets, bank accounts, exploiters
of the masses by the emerging military
industrial complex, as warned by the
Patriot five-star general at the end of
a second term, and the veteran of PT 109
appealed, working in the best interest of all
citizens of America, to keep the influence of
Decisions by the self-governed, when to commit
our personnel to the defense of the original
Idea when threatened by foreign and
domestic enemies to the rule of law and
order, where no one is above
another, all are heard, even the
Absurd, the Bush wars, the first
by chicanery, the second perpetuated by
the lore of blind faith, the cultural corporations
dictatorial monotheism, shades of monarchy
Tyrants none the less, the volunteer force of
America's military might believe in the promise
of a secular, inclusive society, despite the
Inequities created by the benefactors of death, the
profiteering few immersed in greed, the breed of
the inconceivable, irreconcilable, greedy
villain of the highest order, the order of the wealthiest
Minority to subjugate the free-thinking majority with deception
is not the America the veterans fought for, to
risk their livelihoods held in high esteem, not to skirt
their service as the wealthy is known for
profiteering off the backs of those making the ultimate
Sacrifice, non-partisan affiliations,
the sharp pain in the lower body,
the slow descent to the ground, the darkness
beyond self-control, all loved ones
miss your goodbye, the plans you had
for whom you were to become, all of
your cares have gone by, sorrowful loss of joy
this is the last, the end of your

being, maybe there's a train of others to guide
but this stop is where you get off the ride,
It proceeds forever on without you
you hope, thoughts, and prayers deliver you.
The lesson learned all are created equal
"Four score and seven years
ago that government of the people
by the people, for the people,
shall not perish from the Earth."

(*Contains material in the public domain)

Love Amnesia

I'm a real renaissAnce MAN
                    (A)
Living in my   garbage can . . .

If we act sexually
   we are in safe
                    Formal -
Endless. More. Diversity.
         This is of the utmost integrity
      It is the loyal companionship
       it is life itself with endless
            different new experience old
               shared in endless rays
                    of hope, not dope,
                       expressED individually
                          is even endless more
I'm Glad you let
yourself out. Especially now
you should express yourself

I have love amnesia
   I cannot remember a tender moment

ahold of my mother's hand
or the time when I first felt love,

Love amnesia is a lack of love
  Where a woman gives her love by torchlight
  For so long I have been blinded by the dust
    of neglect

I suffer from love amnesia
  I expect to feel competent
  a new life
    the ability to understand true love.

I'm a real renaissAnce MAN
              (A)
Living in my   garbage can . . .

If we act sexually
  we are in safe
              Formal.
Endless. More. Diversity is integrity to the utmost
  It is the loyal companionship
    it is life itself with endless
        different new experience and old
          shared in endless rays
              of hope, not dope,
                  expressED individually
                    is even endless more
                      diversity
I'm Glad you let
yourself out. Especially now
you should express yourself

I have love amnesia
  I cannot remember a tender moment
  ahold of my mother's hand
  or the time when I first felt love,

Love amnesia is a lack of love
  where a woman I love, I forgot, is liberty not given
  For so long, I feel blinded by the dust
    of neglect

I suffer from love amnesia
  I expect to feel competent
  a new life
  the ability to understand true love.

I'm a real renaissAnce MAN
              (A)
Living in my   garbage can,

If we act sexually
  we are in safe
                formal
        Endless More
Diversity is of the utmost integrity
  It is the loyal companionship
    it is life itself with endless
        different new experience and old
        shared in endless rays
          of hope, not dope,
              expressED individually
              is even endless more
I'm Glad you let
yourself out. Especially now
you should express yourself

I have love amnesia
  I cannot remember a tender moment
  ahold of my mother's hand
  or the time when I first felt love

Love amnesia is a lack of love
  her love is not given blindfolded
    For so long I, too, have been blinded by the dust

of neglect

I suffer from love amnesia
    I expect to feel competent
    a new life
        the ability to understand true love.

I'm a real renaissAnce MAN
            (A)
Living in my   garbage can . . .

(12/29/2005)

You Do Not Have To Understand What I Am Saying

You have to understand what I am meaning

When death confronts you with life to remain
    The people of power and money
    Who want to obtain

Become the voices
    Running thee domain
    And everyone else follows

take the sense of being
    Detained
    As nothing less

than people of power
    playing you
    for a fool.

I'm ready to do my best
   What is offered?
   What is to come my way,
   Things I have been bewildered by
      are ranked in the millions
   of years ago, came the greatest challenge
     relinquish to myself my soul
   from the boundaries of mediocracy.
   The way of common life
   It's all it takes to be fulfilled.

Progress

Have you, can you
reach your potential?
To be a professional ballerina
baseball player, athlete
a doctor, a lawyer, an accountant
or any other discipline
All people deserve success
Can't all criminals be poets?
Muses, musicians, or politicians?
Follow your life, your dream
Mysteriously, steps become concrete
does gleam
   (final stanza)
Unlike a dream
 or magic
knowledge is the answer
the democratic theme
marketplace of - ideas -

spur an understanding
   with strength and hype
we see there is an entrance. From the operation
of The Glass Planet:
              < this is it,
"All of the people," this is the saying –
   waking democracy   message
Japanese said, "We have awoken a 'sleeping giant';
That 'sleeping giant' is democracy."
Religion is the only thing
   that can kill us.
The paradox of man's religious beliefs:
Too scared of the future, too sacred
  to face the open, bare depth of the universe
without the support of their God, who
  is astonished to take his believers
   blindly into the promised land of death.
The promise on earth is to live to qualify for
an eternal life in a gated community.
   While wealth and comfort are realized for a few
allows them to enter heaven as likely
as a camel can pass through a needle's eye.
     A finer negotiation could give some love and
  less greed for all before we cash in at the grave.

never felt that I wanted
the mushy clump in my pants
from being afraid of the Republican slant
that wants to kill me
as an American, though I
do not believe in their ranks
I remember when Republicans were
liberal like Abraham Lincoln,
now they are fascist pigs
and want to kill me

Life is too short
to stop living
now as time
slips pass our
heartbeats breathe sight
thinking what we hear
smell taste desire
wish for or lust
love seek and
solve there is
more than perceived to
reach for
inside out
too long to
pass on.

Ten Steps

before you take another
is not a commandment
though you must know
those who believe
in blind faith
will make you
follow.

I cannot do any more
the time has come when I am unable to perform
in any way but humility
need I say more
other than saying
that two points in contention
if you plan to quit
or if you are forced to quit
the difference is your will
versus the conditions that
disable you.
It will be the conditions
that disables you from
expression
It will be your will
to make it happen

Somewhere, Sometime

My life is a big blob of jelly
    I quiver, blood pulses, heartland races
    My legs quiver when crossed
    my teeth gently brush across

White walled rooms in any city
    with any people, friends only
    I stand above myself and the others
    in my view, I see love amongst us all

Idealism, liberal virtues in theory
    are weak, my views are about love, friendship
understanding with taste
    my flavor is not universal, unfortunately

The world is not too romantic
    every hope of every person achieved
    how boring, yet we deceive ourselves
    eternally nothing is about me

Eternity is about everyone
    my love is not defined by me solely
neither friendship nor understanding
    yet within my world, I see the answers

The real answers are those
    which allows you and everybody
to meet me somewhere, sometime.
    Beyond our time here, complacent living while dead

All it takes is everything to see everything to love it all to
    understand its origins
    It's as easy to see as a spade, a diamond, a heart, or a club
    of royalty

Everyone on this planet is a genius of love
    all it takes is to love everything
    in respect to the rareness of
    the fragility of existence

Let Freedom Reign

The Continuous Spontaneous Instant
here now gone
Forever to rise again
mostly without me
Fill the moment with
all you can

We are living in a time of gush it;
this is all bullshit.
In modern times, this is what I see:
We are created equal.
we are all different and free
there is no guarantee
of fairness. From this point
on, life is as uncertain
as it will ever be,
there is always a point
 in destiny, when everything
    equals changes.

It does not
matter what
you believe in
America, but that
you can express
it, when you do
democracy puts it all out there
and the **Second Amendment** is also there
if WORDS (*First Amendment*)
are not enough
to speak justice to power
(but metal shattering
bullets were
not predicted.) It was

"Fire when you see the whites of their eyes!"
Words were mightier than the sword -

Until the money divides us
power supersedes democracy
fight and distract each other,
the money grubber says!

Those who pay for the wealthy's riches are you, us, all
Without you, us all the money grubbers
Would have no capability to gain
Power without you, us, we all pay our

Share of taxes, yet when the
wealthy gain office
You, we, we all pay for their tax -
cuts a lot for the wealthy

May freedom in liberty sustain
to the point of taking the notion
Them, they, the wealthiest, are greed-
fascist, a sickness of the ego, a crime
to Humanity and one that
You, we, we all can be cured by taking office
from township to city to state to country
United States of America~ God Bless thee!

The spirit of life has
Rescinded from within me
The glossing youth
Chiseled and cooled
Like the blacksmith's irons
A welded form of beauty
From silversmiths
Sturdy to the end.

There is more
Than one
Taste

To everything.
~~Except World~~
Accept World
Peace.

(2/23/1994)

I Sing It In My Brain

Don't forget,
I am old
fashioned – I walk
on my own
two feet
and I sing
a tune
in my brain
as I parade
through our
flower garden
circus:

And about all
present nature
and about all
the Flowers
and amongst all
the Flowers
and within all
the Flowers

I Sing It In My Brain

the integrated brilliance
magnificence
of all shades
of color
when warm and
well nourished
as we are left singing
breathing deeply in

the scented airs of what is wild   31
    breathing peaceful pollen
        lusty pollen floating
        shimmering, bristling blindly

        about us
            amongst us
                within us

I Sing It In My Brain

    the integrated brilliance
We are made to walk
    in the wild air
        strolling hand in
hand with the only concern
        of our origin being the same
        May our seeds of the heart
            stay rooted in this
        fertile union
        and forever

    ,to see about us
        ,to speak amongst us
            ,to feel within us

            the people's reign goes on.

We are an excellent learning machine
    the intellectual
machine doesn't want to get too
    far ahead
For if they do
we will
catch
up with
them
It would be their end.

My hurt is experienced
   Determined outward
   As deeply as it
   Is rooted within

So, speak
   to me
   and I will
   listen
And then
we will be
   friends.

        Strolling hand in
hand with the only concern
   Of our origin being the same
   May our seeds of the heart
      stay rooted in this
  fertile union and forever
To see about us
    ,to speak amongst us
    ,to feel within us

   the people's reign goes on.

don't translate my experience
to conform to your machinations
my need from you is to kiss me
   I will be a force sent
with you, I can be fantastic
   as a man
for the first time, I have
   tasted the crust of your life

you are for me
   all that encompasses life
   Liberty, freedom, happiness
   Lover's love
   frailty, sturdiness, and strength

intelligence, affection, and attitude
You're beautiful radiance
  wide eyes wise

the moonbeam smiles
resplendent
alive
  vibes.
I do not believe
  in the afterlife
I do not care
  for all that

I believe in life
  now, love now
the recognition
  of all people as
full of potential
    mysterious
uniquity
    let freedom reign!

Let Freedom Reign   (11/5/2011 11:31 PM)
    has cracked
the bond. Their oath of
  democracy, one of
the pillars of the
    American Experience
  is the free exchange
of ideas and arguments
amongst the people,
decided by the
people, the 99%
Americans
  who out number
the 0.5 percent
the fair use of

shared wealth without the practice of
Imperialism.

We need to support the future
generations, they are the future,
we are dying, we are mortal, it's
about the future generations, it's not
always also

I've seen a lot of odd couples, opposites
I hope that can happen to me
I fear what laziness I might have to suffer
Luck into a beautiful woman for me!

She's pretty, she's liberty, opportunity for all!

(4-22-09 11 PM)

        democracy! Don't jump, democracy! (3-11-25)
        It's going to be alright ~
        It's what is expected from the mentally
        ill health, wealth to power with the mind of a

five-year-old child, abandoned of their childhood ~ unlike
   Rosebud
   who knows disgrace

You, too, remember when sunshine shone
shown, relentless, to pursue intolerance
from your classroom of human conscience
with the broom of decency and self-respect

sweep out the cobwebs of generational dysfunctions
of suspicion, hate, and greed ~

Bonds of faith vary in democracy! Don't jump, democracy!
It's going to be alright ~
  the faith in human diversity is nature's choice
to overcome the adversities, we face in the fight to survive

within nature herself. Identify your strengths and improve
your weaknesses to strive for the 'well-being' of the human
condition

You, also, remember when sunshine shone
shown, relentless, to pursue intolerance
from your classroom of human conscience
with the broom of decency and self-respect
sweep out the cobwebs of generational dysfunctions
of suspicion, hate, and greed ~

The future is present: "Psyche" asteroid 16, potential for
a healthier wealth for everyone to benefit
prosperity, knowledge, and opportunities are
abundant, endless to people provided with

the basic amenities of relief from need or want.
No desperation: The endorsement of the idea is universal.

The right to life, liberty, and the pursuit of happiness ~

Economics supports the economic well-being by supporting
proponents of wealth.
        The well-being of the Earth's occupants is dependent
upon full nourishment, shelter, clothing, medicine, toys, security,
hope, and acceptance ~

In the true and obedient heart, all that is human is never
out of style, only anger and hate. Neuroses are a dis - ease
                of the Conscience ~

The fish pool with the piranhas.
        The whimsical blow-off of the palm
                The thought is in touch with time -

Let Freedom Reign

Until the money divides us
power supersedes democracy

fight and distract each other,
the money grubber says!

Those who pay for the wealthiest riches is you, us, all
Without you, us, all the money grubbers
Would have no capability to gain
Power

Without you, we all pay our
Share of Taxes, yet when the
wealth gains office
You, we, we all pay for their tax -cuts
 Bust the plot of the wealthy

Let Freedom Reign

liberate to the point of taking the notion
them, they, the wealthiest, are greed-
fascist, a sickness of the ego, a crime
against Humanity, one that
you, us, we all can cure by taking office
from city to state to country

United States of America~ God Bless thee!
The United States of
America, a
land of unparalleled
diversity. A payoff of the
unimaginable sickness.

   Every real American
knows of the strength
of the diversity of these lands,
Alaskan Mountains to the Hawaiian Islands,
from the open expanse of
 fields, prairies

Arkansas, across the Midwest, Kansas, Oklahoma
straight out to Nebraska,

the deep, sultry Alabama, Mississippi,
wet heat, agriculture to swamps,
with stately homes to la maison from New
Orleans to Savannah, Georgia
charm of Charleston, South Carolina, Raleigh,
North Carolina, Richmond, Virginia
Maryland, Pennsylvania, Delaware
who takes umbrage

to the Northeast, sharing hurricanes, tornadoes,
the humid air, the dry sticks of the six in
New England, New York, New Jersey,
Florida summers are tropical there, too
a chance for snow with a quick splash
of Spring, life pops into bloom

with thunderstorms to Autumn, a dusting of
dried leaves, harvest moons, and meals,
Minnesota, the Dakotas, Wisconsin, Idaho
the chimney with lumber smoke
fills the air across Michigan, Illinois, and Indiana
Ohio, Missouri, Kentucky, Tennessee, Louisiana

Texas wide as the eye can see to New Mexico
Arizona, Utah, Nevada four corners meet,
sky slumber dormancy wields deserts in
Big Sky states: Wyoming, Montana, and Iowa
Colorado, west to the California Pacific
coastal pacifies Oregon, Washington with rain.

   naked pine forests stand
tall into the late darkness
where survival is close-knit and cozy
  Union of States, home of the brave
              land of the free who
    Let Freedom Reign!

President's Peril

Three of the four assassinated in office fought corruption, backed
civil rights, and the fourth supported the Gilded Age. Three held
high aspirations, overcoming skeptics, the fourth favored the
elites, ignoring rights. The only incumbent wounded opened
corporate flood gates; the two former chief commanders wounded
are polar opposites when it comes to integrity, morality,
sophistication of EQ, and IQ. The lowest won their campaign;
while threats, plots, and attempts foiled were launched against
fourteen, some were for their progress in advancing the American
Dream, fewer were for their incompetence. All were unpopular
with some, while none were popular with all. Peril threatened by
psychopaths or political strife did not prevent saving the Union or
landing on the moon.

[Unbridled Love]

Anyone who loves life
Will be open with their heart
to accept what is in existence
for it is all a miracle
Any of us is here to
experience the joys of freedom,
 to love, to procreate, to build
an aesthetic beneficial to all
 it is desired
Remember, life is as beautiful
 as it is fragile and only
as real as you can imagine
 it can be done.
Enraged observers disagree
The survival of the fittest
     Adopted from wildlife
Obscene is mean is weak
Obtain a brain a claim

Observe the folly the vulnerability
Random activity if not organized in the brain
Even on a farm, a field, or
   a block of land
No classifications
   No discriminations
      or rude interruptions
Here is a place of circumstance
   where evidence of your growth
      told a truer story
Then the present place of your
      emotional state solid unpleasant is
intolerance of God-given differences
I am revealing myself to you
   moments of truth shared with you
carrying me across the frontier
I stopped to stare at the horizon
   I dare to dream of hardiness, purity, vigilance
stopping to stare without expectation at the horizon
      I dare to dream of valor, innocence, justice
believing in times to be, times shared
   for me, what it is all about
         today, now, fire, passion, love
Perseverance to responsibility
      is in the doing,
            not in the saying
Red, White, and Blue

Sing Them Your Heart Song

Remember come January
twentieth at noon
I pledge to the flag
The air will turn
foul, tridactyl hallux eagle will
take flight, soaring to
the skies ~
       Pronounce your
fury now, schedule that date!
  July 4th, 1776
Sing now, free one,
Before the tide rolls in
       Sing them your
Heart song
       Bring praise to
your being exulted
       Condemn the malicious behavior
of the perverted, angry
confused and ignorant
fear from
       tomorrow promises
nothing yet a gleam
in the eye for a better
future for all.

(Original ©1994; 12/14/24)

Give Me Two Pieces Due! 41

Is there nothing smaller
My tender love, who thinks
being is greater than being there
Give me two pieces due!
(some sort of good thing happens)
Moving forward without doubt!
   bricks and a stone
land on your thoughts
giving a flow to everyone

Dad, I know my position
as a fourteen-year-old may
seem inconsequential to you,
but I retain as a naturally inherited
right, that I can educate myself as
I grow older. What can you say to that? Huh?
"You are a F-ing brat, F-ing muskrat?"
I want to love you the most I can before I die.
       I don't want to die for a long time.

We should forever hope
that all our childhoods
Are fairytales
indulge with duly love
we are capable of it – for everyone ever
born. Don't give up on
our democracy, boy,
Its good points are the

tremendous creations by which a free range
– of thoughts occur
All of life has a separate identity
unto itself
brings inspiration, ambition, and hope
    love is where all other truths are between
      us exists ending
        only in the

yet hope happy and well for socialism,
    you might as well throw in Eastern philosophy
    as there's always a need for generosity
       compassion blinds the deafest of the wealthy

    enabling the weak to be strong
       the dreams to be dreamt
       the sun to be the moon
         and the moon to be the sun

    so be the girl
        whose gusto becomes
a brave, strong woman
    of everything

rain, snow, or shine
    I will deliver
    I know where you're at in
       your life, my dear

    You're dueling with tidal waves
       of emotion, in an instant, bleak,
    A moment faltered at the first weakness
       Expectation is only a dream

An evolution of me
my brain dreams of times present
past incarnating the growing
reality of life

it expands, creating new realities
never known before incorporating
my brain awake knows not what it fears
    until what it fears makes itself present

    Provoked emotions act on instinct
    Ask questions, learn lessons later
    My brain dreams of the future
       of times never to be

       listening, nevertheless, I cannot help it

dreams are an evolution of me
Give me life, give me life
     Just remember

          My moments are for
          Real
     they are
          Forever

Beverly Road
"D" train
Flatbush
In our little homes

Children's imaginations run
     wild, creating towns of green and
     blue from the objects in
          their room, in the room itself,

          very
                    many
                         cities
                              thrive.

The New American Love

Passion, we press to join
With one another
Our differences separate us
Our individuality
draws us near
We are merging
For the better of our
Consciousness

> I hate you!
>
> > I hate you!

But the universe is big
Bigger than any of us
Unless we are together
As one, it is so that we continue
On our fateful merger

> They are responsible,
> > They who oppose us!

We must combine
  Join forces, for against
them, we fight to survive!
Guilt is never imminent
When we join to understand
Who we are
Our friction is greater than

> Any single fault
> > on any Richter scale

A diving board leading the
grace of fondness
into the pool of
bright tingling
  bold love
mingling the touch,
of fingertips, tongues
        lips
  happiness of humanity
it is as new old as old new it is.

Human Race, Full Of Contents

Have all of our ingredients
been fully disclosed?
 those nutrients of
a secret sauce that flavors
our taste buds clamor
to a tingle, a touch
of tongue to flesh

ourselves with fear
to taste the fullness
racing flows thick like
lava all time slows
loving never too much
resigning always too soon
 rings in a never-ending

cycle of pleasure and pain
of dreams and nightmares
of breeding and annihilating
of cultivating and purging
of living and dying
riding stampedes smothered
by flowers in blossom

To cease the unrelenting
ongoing of age and demise,
be me for once and know
what it is to die,
a fear beyond truth
a truth beyond fear
to know what the end is

A beginning of something again,

I like smelling flowers,
 only when it's

(5/29/2017, 3 PM)

not my garden,
a lot more than when
the flowers
are in my own

The garden is forever
or until the sun shines too hot
garden is, and will be forever
    or the cloudy rains are too wet
    when our love may shrivel and die
on soak to drown in

The scent of flowers
    remaining strong
    now our garden is gone
wasted in ways never wasted before
    in never seen before wasted ways
eaten by us, hushed by the itch
    of wayward tyranny

There's an Indian smoking pipe in my drink
Messiah by listening to music "hits tape"
as some songs are about peace or power
are about the Messiah
up with these songs.
Other songs are included,
the makers of myth

The eternal fate of human existence
    is dependent on the actions
    of the whole existence past into
    the most important present.
    The good, saintly deeds
    of the heroic, brave
    actions by us

The evil, inhuman
    unspeakable acts performed

of cowardice, greed,
weak-minded avarice
will amount to hatred
    the defining moment
of our final outcome

prevails with strength
of conviction for the
common good.
My being is as
 equal to any others
the terms and conditions that
apply are based on . . .

(2-23-02)

Loving and Knowing
 are two beautiful
concepts in the
 world, a part of
having a conscience.
 Human, a soul of sorts
with a recognition character

 of abilities separate from
other living forms
 not always superior, mind you
how many other living
 beings, species, actually
cook thin food?

 Hope is in every species alive
or extinct enjoys-ed
 sex, the only other mutual
 attribution beyond food,
 sex will be in security
done by force
by force security will be done in goodwill

Purple Hands Happenstance

       Of freezing culprits huddled
on desert curbs of solid sand
       (praying Jesus didn't die
in vain)
       Praying, (knowing) Jesus
didn't die in vain
Praying (knowing) Jesus did
not die in vain
With Bethlehem
  and Jerusalem
  like Washington D.C.,
it's a place for
its' professionals
for all others to visit.
Modernize or
Lock-down
Law with Order
or an Anarchy-Chaos
Civilize or
Die-off
Choose Love to
  End-Hate.
Out of (action)
the effect of gravity on
immobile objects, with or without
gravity to assist in the object's
    mobility.
There is Evil
because . . .
. . . there is gravity.
Evil is an extreme for you
      of gravity in or out of action
with or without intent.
With intent:
HATE + Anger

Intellectual and
emotional
   freedom. In
place is anxiety
      fear weighing down
   the conscience

The Fear Of Obscurity

The hardships
of life develops
human character.
When you don't apply
yourself willfully, your luck
privilege, spoiled brat.

Titty-baby, the opportunity
to become a stronger
person from within; The
reasoning and rationale of love
is more than a story told
in a book.

Love is limitless when reciprocated,
when not, then it is another lesson
to revisit the inner core of reasoning,
 rationale builds the aesthetic of love
continuously to yourself over again
in defining adjustments made to find
common sense.

Melting

I think we're
  together,
a hot knife through
  a warm stick
of butter. Melting
victory laps are cool, no matter what
          shape you're in
all of a sudden, somebody wants to become
          a star
    a workout,
you need an ego boost or a nice
      day out in the sun, various
        beauties of the day, the champagne flows
    in full summer spirit
heat off the pavement crisscrosses by a
    cool, subtle breeze, a wind whirling
      from a lake, tandems ride by
        flocks of birds singing
              child's chorus alone in
        a sight no other person can see
              charms of color blue, green, purple,
          brown, black, white,
                red, orange, and yellow are crisp, clear-cut
        of the multitude of shades,
              I see people melting hot
      stickered suitcases by the globe
          some remain cool under family
      trees, others, unreal bind birds
            on the lake, the same as
    one's expected they never
            make any noise or hear
      the towering buildings
            over Central Park reflecting
      in the lake behind
              metal, glass, cement trees

the blue-sky light travels shorter, smaller waves
    dark clouds, gray tumultuous
the water is juicy, rolls and curls reflecting
    sparkling of thought pollution
my bench is hard
    my ass hurts
by the wings of the jet
    looking out of the porthole
there we were
    fucking ducks dying
before our Eyes
    a well-built goddess
watches over liberty's torch
    resort to this because
the human existence
    gets blinded by comfort
that gods forget
    while the devils
rarely do.
    While the rested
legends of mythology
    begets a child
of humility, reticent of humor
    She redescends proclaiming
Her justice is for all those melting

Greenwich Village Is The Belly of Jelly

A sundown or a sunrise
 somehow the place smells of wooden
oak whiskey (or is it forgotten dreams?)
that linger of faithful nights into
truthful days

somehow, somewhere
I distinguish where this taste
    sour and sweet in my mouth
 comes from a Wild Turkey's
beak comes from

Yes, yes, I see it now
How you were standing on the
sidewalk while I was drunk
    you were scheming
    to lure me in

you wanted to screw me
in my mind
    to smell the taste
of pizza drew me away
    only because . . . because loneliness

Greenwich Village is a festival
    of love, if I use the word
        again, I will kill myself
slowly,
    ounce by ounce

Gay persons, bi-queer-trans- persons,
    People here, yet there, wherever you
        may live in the land
of the free, welcome home of the brave
    to love beyond personal affections for

the brave of freedom gives way to garrulous gossip
  skip a rock on a pond
before following it to plunk.
  This was, or is, the mother of nature,
to let freedom reign, an easier score for all of us to find

Who knows how god wants me to live?
  Who knows what god has in store for me?
All I know is that god, existence
  doesn't know me, entirely.
I know you better than you know me!

the loss of Innocence
  Epic Times
sex burning on a sidewalk
  I love my time on this earth
I know I am, what are you?

She finds insights
  making love between us
happens, never forget the ones
  you love, by being there
forever it takes the first time

Never forget the ones you love.
  Life's light indulgences do not compare
    when you remember meaning
  in the worlds to investigate,
    the eyes, voice, the mind in the moment

    When I do see the macro in the micro
    thank you, my friend, ethical, honest
    this hour speaks with conviction, urges
    desires, I love strength of courage denies,
      fearing the growth of ostracization

son, I stumble end over
  knot the bond
    naught but together me
     not over our differences
      nor to the blood we bleed

I'm me Metaphysical person
  I'm an Existentialist philosopher
   I'm a Transcendentalist spirit
    romanticism,
     experience,

heart beating, lungs breathing,
  mind thinking, increasing with each day
   more tolerance each day
    anyway, beautiful each day
  growing every day!

(7/25/2009 11:39 PM; 5/18/25 4:04 PM)

Reprise The Commander Of Love

Yell in command:
    Fire!   Love!
    Fire!   Love!
    Fire!   Love!
Our forces advance on the enemy of acceptance
   Before the top hat of their intolerance
     Succumbs to toppling off
We give every offer to join us in being in charge
    large enough to fit all time, history, knowledge, spirit
     love into every moment of being.

(4/18/25/4:16 PM)

When The Sun Shines Brightly, One Needs

time to absorb it in, for fifteen
minutes per day
Smart ladies carry umbrellas, expecting

some	colorful,	diverse,	and	bright,
some	delicate,	delightful,	and	fashionable,
some	creative,	fun,	and	gay,
some	strung,	charismatic,	and	genius,
some	brave,	women,	and	impoverished,
some	loving,	children,	and	mindful,
some	scared,	men,	and	beards,
some	sturdy,	family,	and	arguing,
some	frightful,	zombie,	and	drunk,
some	addict,	addiction,	and	addicted,
some	politics,	dead,	and	noise,

When the sun shines brightly, one needs
time to absorb it in, for fifteen
minutes per day
protection, sincerity, bleed,
sacrifice, commitment, [need](.)
Smart ladies carry umbrellas, expecting,
their opinions of the storm
are taken in heed! (3-1-2021; 8:15 AM)

Lonely In A Big City

Walking down one of the common streets of New York City
I see you passing
I see your sad eyes
I see you looking into my eyes
I see you glancing away

Walking down one of the common Avenues of New York City
I feel you pass me
I feel your sadness as lights glitter in your eyes
I feel your isolation when avoiding my eyes
I feel you, I feel the cold city's embrace

Walking down one of the anonymous sidewalks of New York City
I pass you with a feeling, without your feelings
I pass you with an understanding, without understanding you
I pass you, grabbing your life, without knowing your life
I pass you silently, as you pass me ever more silently

Walking down one of the incredibly populated passageways of
    New York City
I become enchanted with our surroundings, almost surreal
I become fascinated with our indifferent attitude towards the
    multitudes, multitudes, multitudes . . .
I became overwhelmed with the visions of idealism and the feeling
    of decadence,
I become in this moment everything you want me to be,

A Strange Mangled Roar *

The father and child who inspect the 1950s pickup truck in the
barn, the grassy fields, and the rusty tractor from yesteryear;
The memories of those who died for this day;
the plate glass holds the negatives of the deaths from the homeland
war, more deaths than all the wars together, to the greenery, the
botanical gardens, with lilacs in mind, flowers for the headstones,
the greenhouse, the ferns sway with the tall grass, the panes
memories fade away in the shine of the sun's rays;
The better angels beat the draft dodgers.
The patriots, the Union soldiers, USCT;
The Rough Riders;
 the Doughboys; the Buffalo Soldiers; Harlem Hellfires; Blue
Helmets; the 761st Tank Battalion; the Tuskegee Airmen; 24th
Infantry Regiment; 2nd Ranger Infantry; Triple Nickels; the G.I.s;
the industrial military service people, all of the military mighty
forces; the criminal, desperate, without recourse, having never
received a course of study, any reason for not taking a course, or
lessons learned to take another generation's no choice in the
matter
born without asking, the living must provide what is necessary
no excuse, law and order
no excuse, opportunities created for the one percent who serve,
no excuse, day to day, to be a work in progress, life always
challenges to circumstances unforeseen, here is the crux, winning
is not a victory when due process is neglected. Life is not a
sentence for the misfortunate, ignorant, or stupid, we do not ask
to be born, we do not ask to have to die.
The human experience is dependent on the caring for each other
without the vices of indifference, no discrimination, no
judgements on one's station in society, for no one has sole
providence, understanding, or knowing the circumstances of fate
dealt to a stranger, their courage, surprise, and fear are not to be
measured on the scales of uninterpreted injustice.

(*Contains material in the public domain)

Imagine A World

Nano size to test healthiness
Fashion turns into protection
Autonomous materials
Self-organize
> move
> > sense
> > > Respond
Energy and power to make things move –
horses have driven human innovation for millennia
Harness it!
Synthesize it!
From biological to human-made
Innovate it!
> – replicate to build upon.

Energy and Power to make things move
- Bacteria swarming – active matter
- turbine is being rotated by bacteria turning it

(forces our distance = work)
to bring biology

- man-made version – synthesize it.
- Turbines to free synthetic swimmers.

Where are we going – miniature size it.
nano-scale machine
made of protein
- All bodily activity
- affected by protein

The enzyme takes in the molecule
turns it into a new molecule.
- Enzymes for Energy
- – can we do it?

fuel, energy – exhaust
Contradicts Einstein's theory
- no theory needed

to be organ eyes.
At the beginning of the present
-   Heal wounds by growing cells on tissue
    that can heal itself
-   Control – as potholes are occurring
    they repair themselves.
-   Sense + Respond – Venus fly trap senses touch
    a dreamer makes the clothes.

What is wrong?
what is wrong?
With the sky so perfect.
The clouds, the sun, the blue sky
the winds' breath is robust
the eagle soured after time
        rescinds from the laws of flight.

What is wrong?
  With the oceans, seas, rivers, and lakes
  the fish swim, eat
        sea urchins
    surviving in the depths below
    the micro-plastics
feed and are fed

What is wrong?
  With the forest, mountains, deserts, jungles,
  the creatures
        go to undress
    claiming
      homes
        to die in

When the gifts of a virtuous expanse
      turn to waste
    in pursuit of happiness
      of a few in blind belief
    of a manifest destiny
        they find no one stands
      above the law of the land

THE END

Remember those citizen heroes
who made the ultimate sacrifice
in defense of democracy
and the secular government
of the people, by the people, for the people

Memorial Day   July 4th   Veterans Day
1776 - 2026